HMR Diet

A Review, Analysis, and Beginner's Overview of the Diet Program

copyright © 2019 Bruce Ackerberg

All rights reserved No part of this book may be reproduced, or stored in a retrieval system, or transmitted in any form or by any means, electronic, mechanical, photocopying, recording, or otherwise, without express written permission of the publisher.

Disclaimer

By reading this disclaimer, you are accepting the terms of the disclaimer in full. If you disagree with this disclaimer, please do not read the guide.

All of the content within this guide is provided for informational and educational purposes only, and should not be accepted as independent medical or other professional advice. The author is not a doctor, physician, nurse, mental health provider, or registered nutritionist/dietician. Therefore, using and reading this guide does not establish any form of a physician-patient relationship.

Always consult with a physician or another qualified health provider with any issues or questions you might have regarding any sort of medical condition. Do not ever disregard any qualified professional medical advice or delay seeking that advice because of anything you have read in this guide. The information in this guide is not intended to be any sort of medical advice and should not be used in lieu of any medical advice by a licensed and qualified medical professional.

The information in this guide has been compiled from a variety of known sources. However, the author cannot attest to or guarantee the accuracy of each source and thus should not be held liable for any errors or omissions.

You acknowledge that the publisher of this guide will not be held liable for any loss or damage of any kind incurred as a result of this guide or the reliance on any information provided within this guide. You acknowledge and agree that you assume all risk and responsibility for any action you undertake in response to the information in this guide.

Using this guide does not guarantee any particular result (e.g., weight loss or a cure). By reading this guide, you acknowledge that there are no guarantees to any specific outcome or results you can expect.

All product names, diet plans, or names used in this guide are for identification purposes only and are the property of their respective owners. The use of these names does not imply endorsement. All other trademarks cited herein are the property of their respective owners.

Where applicable, this guide is not intended to be a substitute for the original work of this diet plan and is, at most, a supplement to the original work for this diet plan and never a direct substitute. This guide is a personal expression of the facts of that diet plan.

Where applicable, persons shown in the cover images are stock photography models and the publisher has obtained the rights to use the images through license agreements with third-party stock image companies.

Table of Contents

Introduction   7
Quick Look into What HMR Does   10
   HMR and Weight Loss   10
   The Claim   11
   Theoretical Support   11
Deep Dive into HMR   12
   HMR as Number 1 "Best Fast Weight-Loss Diet"   13
   Basics of HMR   13
   Meal Replacements   14
   Exercise   15
Pros and Cons of the HMR Diet   16
   The Good Side of HMR   16
   Potential Health Benefits of the HMR Diet   18
   The Downside of HMR   20
   Health Concerns of the HMR Diet   22
How HMR Works   24
   Phase One: Quick Start Phase   25
   Phase Two: Transition Phase   30
HMR Nutritional Information   33
   Conformity to the Dietary Guidelines   33
   How Much Does HMR Cost   36
Is It Worth It?   39
Correcting Misconceptions and Addressing FAQs   41
Conclusion   46
References and Helpful Links   48

Introduction

Not everyone is familiar with HMR, but the majority, especially the millennials and Gen Z, have heard of a diet that makes use of meal-replacement shakes. A lot are skeptical about it. Is it possible to replace meals with a beverage? Will you get sufficient vitamins and nutrients from that? Will you not get hungry without heavy meals? Does it mean you can skip the exercise?

There are many questions and misconceptions about the "meal replacement shake diet". If you do your research, though, you will realize that that particular diet that has gained recent popularity is called the Health Management Resources Diet, or simply, HMR.

Health Management Resources Diet (HMR) was originally formulated about 30 years ago with the main goal of helping obese people lose weight. It is a medically supervised type of Very Low-Calorie Diet or VLCD. Weight loss from the HMR program is achieved by eating very low quantities of calories each day. This creates a calorie deficit that drives metabolism.

HMR is not as well-known as other similar types of weight loss diet because it is originally reserved for in-clinic services, and is catered to those who are clinically obese or are in need of losing more than 40 pounds of excess weight. These people need a more intensive weight loss program and mostly require close supervision for effective and safe weight loss.

This guide will help you understand how and why exactly HMR is effective. You will learn about the different phases of HMR and how the entire program works. This guide will also tell you about what nutritional benefits can come from HMR's product range.

What is good about HMR is unlike other weight loss programs, HMR supplies most of the daily food for its participants who opted for the home program. You will not do much shopping or prepare lots of food each day.

Your food will be delivered, and it will be easy to prepare. Shake mixes are already premeasured. Entrees and hot cereals are all pre-packaged, making preparation as simple as putting food inside a microwave oven. Sounds good, right?

This guide was written with the hopes that you, dear reader, will gain insights regarding HMR. With all the questions surrounding this particular diet, there is so much to cover. Each chapter will help you gain more information on the program.

Whether you are reading this to jumpstart your weight loss journey or to help a loved one in his/her choice to try HMR, may you find each page useful? Best of luck on your path to better lifestyle choices!

Quick Look into What HMR Does

HMR stands for Health Management Resources Diet. This relatively new diet regimen is a modification of the VLCD (Very Low-Calorie Diet) plan. In this type of program, the dieter consumes far fewer calories than the dietary recommendations to lose weight.

HMR and Weight Loss

The HMR program provides fewer calories than the recommended amount to encourage weight loss through the dietary process.

The main goal of HMR is to help you lose weight and become fit by simply reducing calorie intake via meal replacement. Also, fruits and vegetables are incorporated into your diet to keep you full, while maintaining the purpose of reducing the number of calories ingested by your body every day.

On top of these, HMR also aims to teach you healthy lifestyle strategies, increase your physical activities, and develop personal accountability.

The Claim

The reality of the matter is that every meal can either help you lose or make you increase in weight. However, people who change their lifestyle through HMR can maintain significant weight loss for a prolonged period. Such a result is produced especially because HMR is facilitated through medically supervised programs, in-clinic, or at-home options.

Theoretical Support

Studies show that among the best methods to lose weight is to consume meal replacements, which is what HMR does. Three times the weight is lost through this method, proving it to be more effective compared to other traditional diets. This is because there is a lower calorie intake in the designed daily meals consisting of shakes, nutrition bars, multigrain hot cereals, and portioned meals that are consumed in place of common heavy meals.

Aside from the meal replacements, eating vegetables and fruits is also recommended. These are low in calories but rich in nutritional food which will displace higher-calorie foods from a diet. By mixing meals with fruits and vegetables, you have a very nutritious diet to help your body in growth and development and to ensure that you do not accumulate a lot of weight at the same time.

Physical exercise is also encouraged in this case to help you build strong bones and aid in food breakdown into energy.

Deep Dive into HMR

Dieters under the HMR program will undergo intensive dieting for 6 weeks. This usually involves some form of liquid fasting. This period is when most of the weight loss happens. After these 6 weeks, the dieter goes on a low-calorie diet, with meals coming from and prepared by HMR.

The HMR program is a long-term weight loss diet plan. It often costs around $1,200 to $1,900 for each diet plan. Dieters pay this amount for long-term use, lasting for about 6 months up to 2 years.

On average, HMR dieters lose 60 pounds in total for the entire program. This is about 5 pounds per month. For a VLCD type of diet, the amount of weight loss is relatively low. However, the cost can be justified by the presence of medical staff that guides the dieter throughout the program to achieve safe weight loss.

Dieters have the option to cancel the program any time they want. However, there are no free samples or money-back guarantees. Individuals also have the option to make separate purchases on different HMR products.

Despite this, HMR claims that the program is not about fast weight loss. There are so many other diets for that. What HMR believes is that safe and sustainable weight loss can only be achieved by changing lifestyles. People who went through the medically supervised HRM program (either in-clinic or at home) were able to lose weight and keep them off for longer compared to people who had rapid weight loss with other diet programs.

HMR as Number 1 "Best Fast Weight-Loss Diet"

Reducing your weight within a short period is not a simple thing. There are several weight-loss diets out there but this one is a big deal. With HMR, you are likely to lose a lot of weight within a short period. It is ideal for people who want to lose 20 or more pounds. It can as well be practiced at home.

Earlier in January 2018, News and World Report released their rankings for 2018's best diets and HMR was ranked as the top best diet plan to lose a significant amount of weight. It has been ranked as the top best diet plan to lose weight for the last three years.

Basics of HMR

HMR program is a combination of partial liquid fasting and eating low-calorie meals, with low-calorie snacks. This diet program is recommended for people whose target weight loss is more than 40 pounds. HMR is similar to other diets such as Jenny Craig, Nutrisystem, and Medifast.

HMR aims to reduce the calorie intake to lose weight and to keep it off. Calorie reduction is through meal replacements with the addition of vegetables and fruits. Dieters are also taught what lifestyle changes to make and how. Physical activity is increased to aid in losing weight. Dieters under the HNR program are also taught personal accountability.

Followers of the HMR diet get their meals delivered to them. There are HMR clinics all over the US that guide dieters throughout the program. There are also home diet programs guided by a qualified and well-trained counselor. Dieters that follow HMR will have a customized meal plan to suit their individual preferences (i.e., vegetarian, lactose-free, etc.) and unique health needs and conditions.

Meal Replacements

Meal replacements are the main driving force for weight loss. Compared to other traditional weight-loss diets, meal replacements in HMR can help lose 3 times more weight than these other diets.

These meal replacements come in various forms. There are low-calorie shakes, multigrain hot cereal, nutrition bars, and low-calorie prepared meals. In addition to these meal replacements, fruits, and vegetables are added. These natural foods are low in calories and help in replacing all other foods that have higher calorie content. With this combination, meals are more filling, more nutritious yet low in calories. Typically, HMR dieters consume about 500 to 1,200 calories each day.

This calorie deficit drives metabolism and promotes more fat-burning. These actions all work together to bring about weight loss.

Exercise

Aside from meals and calorie deficits, HMR also promotes regular physical activity. Exercise is promoted as a means for long-term, sustained good weight management. It does not have to be too strenuous. In HMR, 10-20 minutes of walking each day is enough to achieve and sustain weight loss goals.

Walking is a very popular exercise among HMR dieters. It does not require any warm-up or fancy equipment. Yet, it burns a lot of calories. For a 225-pound individual, it will only take about 36 minutes of walking at an average pace every day to meet the exercise goal. Experts recommend brisk walking for at least 30 minutes to also get the other benefits of exercise such as the lowered risk for cardiovascular diseases and diabetes, increased energy levels, and keeping weight off.

Pros and Cons of the HMR Diet

The HMR diet has its pros and cons. Medical experts have varying opinions about this diet. Some support it. The program even integrates the services of medical personnel to serve as counsel and to guide the dieter throughout the program. A few experts, on the other hand, raised some issues on some of the items on the program.

The Good Side of HMR

HMR is originally intended to help clinically obese people to lose weight. The program was designed to help those who have to lose more than 40 pounds of excess weight safely. The program is under medical counsel and monitoring to ensure that the weight loss is safe.

Meals in HMR are already pre-packaged. All of these HMR products are packed with nutrients such as minerals and vitamins. The products are carefully designed to create a calorie deficit and still provide the body with the nutrients it needs for proper functioning.

For people with no dieting background, designing your meal and exercise plans can do more harm than good. You might be depriving yourself without you knowing it. This is why starting your dieting journey through HMR is safer than doing them yourself.

Everyone who signs up for HMR will receive support from the staff. Medical personnel are available to help in planning the program. They are also there to make sure that the person is following the guidelines and to monitor for responses to the program. Emotional support is also provided by competent professional staff. Weight loss is not just a physical endeavor. It also takes a toll on the emotions. HMR has qualified experts to deal with all issues, whether physical, medical, or emotional.

For most other weight-loss diets, the dieter would have to go through the trouble of shopping for "allowed" foods and ingredients. This includes having to investigate the ingredients in each food time. Sometimes, the dieter would have to go further by investigating the source of the food just to make sure it is within the standards of the weight loss diet.

In HMR, everything is already pre-made. Meals are prepared by a qualified team that makes sure each bit is packed with the right nutrients and with the required calorie counts. That takes a huge load off the dieter. They do not have to keep counting calories before eating and going through all the trouble of adjusting nutrients and calories at each meal. Best of all, meals are delivered right to the homes of diets. Everything is so convenient.

HMR is all about convenience and fast results. However, there's a possibility of people relying too much on pre-packed meals that HMR provides.

Dieters also have the option to go through the program under close medical supervision. They can opt to have in-clinic HMR, where competent staff monitors them every step of the way. However, those who do HMR at home can still obtain support via the HMR hotline. The staff is always available to help them with any questions or concerns. HMR dieters can always count on these professionals to help them deal with everything they experience throughout the whole ordeal.

Potential Health Benefits of the HMR Diet

Several studies exist to support weight Loss through the HMR Diet. Unlike many other weight loss programs, HMR is backed up by several studies and that's why the majority of health experts are likely to support it.

The effectiveness of both the Decision-free Diet and Healthy Solutions has been examined in a couple of studies. The results were examined in several peer-reviewed scientific journals.

Most of them claim that the average weight loss on a healthy solution is 28-37 pounds in a 12-26 week timeframe. It also states that 59-66 percent of that weight loss is maintained up to 7 weeks later. Although the results are impressive, you have to note that the majority of these studies were funded by HMR and perhaps there is a likelihood of interference. It is common knowledge that perhaps even the other weight loss programs provide the same impressive results for their respective funded programs.

What this means is that most HMR meal replacements are vitamin fortified and hence vitamin needs are met and in some other cases exceeded. You are likely to meet all of your body's vitamin and nutrient requirements even when under dietary plans.

Plans also include additional layers of support. Both the plans included in the MHR program incorporate activities, dietary plans, and associated lifestyle canceling to help you live a healthy lifestyle, meet all your body requirements, and still lose a significant amount of weight.

There are exercise activities that are encouraged each day to burn up to 2,000 calories. Other dietary and counseling providers offer up to 50 minutes of group coaching sessions by phone. What this means is that you can either choose to take part in it or not. Decision-Free Diet users have an involuntary coaching session each week that is offered by a health professional at a facility overseeing the program.

The Downside of HMR

For one, HMR is expensive compared to traditional diets. Meals are done by HMR staff, so dieters under the program don't have the liberty to shop around for cheaper ingredients or alternatives. For a complete basic HMR program, individuals would have to spend a minimum of $1,200.

Shedding a lot of money to get your dream body in a self-restrictive manner will make you think twice. Why not just plan the meals yourself and go to the gym? However, remember that HMR provides you with pre-packaged, dietician-approved meals. This means that there's a lot of thinking involved in your meals before they get into your stomach. All you have to do is pay and do it.

The products are all nutritionally dense, and packed with essential minerals and vitamins. However, HMR products are high in soy. A lot of experts in the field are concerned about the soy content. It can be pretty damaging to overall health and nutrition. HMR says that soy won't be much of a concern because the rest of the ingredients of each HMR product are healthy for the body. People who are undergoing chemotherapy are also advised to avoid HMR products to avoid any negative side effects.

HMR severely limits food choices in their products. There isn't much choice for other foods. With this limitation, meals can get monotonous and boring. The meal replacement shakes, in particular, could quickly become boring and unsatisfying, with the same flavor choices for weeks.

Eating in restaurants and similar places is also highly discouraged. Because the diet program is very strict, there is very little chance of getting to eat anything outside of the HMR products. This can work to avoid any temptations to eat something that must be avoided while on the program. But, people can get dissatisfied and depressed quickly about their diet. HMR responds to cases like these by providing emotional support to its dieters.

A program is a form of VLCD. Health experts believe that calorie intake is way too low, going as low as 500 calories a day. These experts believe that too low caloric intake may cause more health problems. But, according to HMR, the meals are packed with vitamins and minerals that can keep the body from any health problems. The energy needed for daily functions would come from fat metabolism induced by the calorie deficit. People who have existing or are at higher risk for heart problems are discouraged from HMR because the severe calorie deficit may worsen their condition.

Based on these mentioned disadvantages, you can see that starting the HMR diet must not be done impulsively. Compared to other diets, the HMR diet involves financial, emotional, and social sacrifices. Whether the pros outweigh the cons are up to you.

Health Concerns of the HMR Diet

The overall nutrient content of the HMR diet is uneven. Several meal replacements are fortified with vitamins and minerals. What this means is that there is a likelihood of uneven nutrient intake. The user is also likely to consume a lot of sodium than the average intake, which is below the upper limit (2300mg)

Several nutrients appear to be inadequate. For example, the average amount of potassium intake was found to be around 2000mg, which is not in the recommended range. The fiber intake was around 13g, which is out of the range.

However, the HMR recommendations vary by calorie needs and organization. The range that most people are allowed to take per day is between 20-35 grams.

Isolation is another case. Avoidance of social interaction can feel isolating at some times. However, if you learned the mechanisms of having healthy eating before landing in social situations, isolation won't be an issue.

Isolation is a good thing that will help you stay on track calorie-wise but it can affect your social life. Mental health and well-being are better than all those other things.

The pressure of having to eat a lot when you're out with your friends can be a burden. Imagine the horror of trying to track your meals' nutritional value as you talk over the tables. Why not try suggesting other fun activities for your next meet-ups? Physical activities like jogging or cycling are some healthy alternatives to the usual brunch or night outs.

With a little bit of compromise and understanding friends, you never have to experience isolation with the HMR diet.

Adaptability in real life is also an additional challenge. The problem with this program is that they don't teach real skills regarding food choice and meal prep. What this means is that when many people reach their weight loss goal, many people tend to forget all about the HMR diet. During the weight loss phase, cooking skills and other important skills are not key. For this reason, after you have achieved your weight loss goal, it may get worse dealing with real-life situations.

A calorie-restricting diet can be hard to maintain in the long run. For people who only want to achieve their "summer body," this won't be a problem. However, this could alarm those who need to maintain a specific weight for health reasons.

Consider investing in healthy cookbooks and fitness magazines. If you're the tech-savvy type, search online for healthy recipes. Cooking is a lifetime skill, when's the best time to start learning it if not now?

How HMR Works

HMR may seem new to a lot of people. It was a program that was developed by Lawrence Stifler some 30 years ago. Stifler was a behavioral psychologist and is the president of the entire HMR program.

Whether opting for a home HMR program or in-clinic, individuals would have to pass through screening tests. These tests determine eligibility and specific weight loss needs. The dieter will then be given an option for what kind of HMR diet is preferred, such as vegetarian, rapid weight loss, etc. The HMR staff will decide if the dieter needs medical supervision based on the chosen type of HMR diet, medical history, and body mass index.

The Home Program under the HMR is also called Healthy Solutions Diet. It has two phases. Going through the diet step by step and separating it into phases is a good way of giving dieters a quick start on their weight loss regimen. People under this program generally do not need to be placed under medical supervision. But, if a person is diabetic and taking diabetic medications, supervision is highly advised.

Phase One: Quick Start Phase

Phase one is also called the Quick Start phase. The goal of this phase is rapid weight loss, losing as much weight as possible (and safely).

Once an individual signs up for the HMR diet, a diet kit is prepared. This kit contains everything that the individual needs for the first three weeks of the program. Fruits and vegetables needed for this period are not provided, however. These will have to be purchased by the dieter on his/her own. The food provided for by the HMR will arrive at the dieter's home every two weeks. The delivery system is efficient enough to ensure that there is a continuous supply of HMR-approved food. The program is well aware that running out of food will interrupt the weight loss process and they make sure this does not happen.

The food kit contains shake mixes, hot cereals, and entrees. These are already shelf-ready so there is no need to bother with refrigeration and stuff. The hot cereals and entrees are also packed in microwave-ready containers. The individuals are also left free to decide the number of shakes to consume in a day.

For Phase One, the daily diet plan is referred to as "3-2-5". The HMR dieter will have to drink at least 3 HMR shakes, then take 2 HMR entrees, and have 5 1-cup servings of vegetables and fruits. If the dieter is still hungry, he or she can still eat more of these foods. These are considered low-calorie, so it's allowed. Even with the additional servings, the dieter is still expected to lose some weight.

Shakes are the most convenient and the main source of energy in this phase. The shake mixes are delivered right to the participant's home. Making them in a blender is more filling. This may require the participant to bring blenders to work or blend the shakes at home and pour them into a thermos and then bring them along.

Aside from fruits and vegetables, there are a few items that are allowed to be added to the HMR products during this phase. Items include mustard, sugar-free gelatin mix, spices, salsa, diet sodas, and vanilla extract.

One of the most common issues is getting easily bored eating the same meals over and over. In a very low-calorie diet, there's a high possibility of cravings and binge eating. After eating monotonous food for so long, all you want to do is eat something more savory and different. However, don't worry. HMR already saw this problem coming, and they have a solution for that.

HMR allows mixing and matching its various HMR products to keep meals more interesting.

Have HMR pre-packaged foods, prepared vegetables, and fruits always on hand. This greatly helps in staying within the diet. When hunger strikes, there will be HMR food and approved food readily available to satisfy hunger and energy needs. This reduces the temptation of reaching for unhealthy foods.

Starting at Phase One, all fast-food entrees must be avoided, including restaurants and coffee shops. This may be difficult but it has to be done. To make it easier to stay away from these places, a dieter may have to give up some of his/her social activities.

Limit social functions that involve food

Physical activity is also part of Phase One. The goal of adding exercise is to induce rapid calorie burning. The optimum goal is to burn 2,000 calories per week. Spread exercise throughout the day. It does not have to be done all at once. Exercise may be moderate to intense like walking, dancing, using the treadmill (set at a moderate pace), and swimming.

Tracking is also part of the program. Weekly progress charts are filled in to track what foods were eaten and how much exercise was done.

Aside from the severe reduction in calories and exercise, Phase one of the QuickStart phase is when the dieter starts to learn strategies for a healthier lifestyle. Professional staff will help the dieter to make the transition towards healthier living. Strategies will be taught and the staff is ready to help in case any trouble arises.

There is no specific time limit to Phase One. The cue that a dieter is ready to proceed to Phase Two is when the goal weight is achieved or when the person is ready for a less structured diet. But, despite the absence of a time frame, there is a target rate of weight loss. Per week, the HMR dieter should lose about a pound or two. The average weight loss should be 23 pounds within the first 12 weeks of the program.

Things to note for this phase

One thing that you need to note at this phase is that drinking alcohol and smoking is highly discouraged. If you get drunk you are likely to make uninformed decisions and in one way or another end up altering the whole process. Smoking or even drinking alcohol is highly linked to weight gain. It is also likely to interfere with the process and the results may not be appealing.

Eating outside is also prohibited during phase one of HMR. If you have to eat outside, ensure that you consume what is recommended and also eat a small amount of it. Taking a break from going to the restaurants during the first few weeks of the program.

Tips to ease into Phase One

In some cases, it may not be possible to eat at home. Perhaps you are on a tour out and the only choice available is to eat at one of the restaurants on your way. However, if you have to eat outside, these tips are going to help you.

Plan ahead - Several restaurants have their menus posted online, look at them and decide on what to consume there. Look for a meal that you are acting on. If possible, call in advance and ask if that serving is available and if they can preserve some for you.

Eat before you go - The other good thing that you can do is to eat before you go. This will ensure that you eat the right amount and the quality that is recommended for weight loss during phase 1. Have a shake or an entrée served with vegetables before you get to the restaurant. What this means is that you will be full and less likely to consume a lot from the hotel.

Carry entrees and shakes with you - There are several restaurants out there that are happy to heat your entrée or even make a shake for you. You can carry your shakes and entrees at room temperature or even ask the waiter/waitress for the service.

Make a meal out of healthy side dishes and salads. If you cannot avoid eating at a restaurant, look for a serving that is less likely to interfere with your main goal of losing weight. Look at a salad and side dishes or vegetables served with something else that you want to consume.

Don't limit yourself to what you see on their menus. If they don't have something that you are acting on, you can move to another restaurant rather than restricting yourself from what you see on the menu. This is likely to interfere with your plans or even make it a difficult move.

Phase Two: Transition Phase

Once a person is ready, Phase 2 commences. This is referred to as the transition phase. It typically lasts from 4 to 8 weeks. Exercise and weekly food tracks continue.

The difference is in the food. HMR foods are still part of the diet plan, with the same amount of vegetables and fruits, at 35 servings per week. HMR food arrives every month. The dieter is now allowed to work with other foods outside of the HMR product range. Start gradually adding non-HMR foods that are healthy and low in calories.

Take a minimum of 14 HMR foods per week while eating foods of your own choice. Focus on eating lean proteins like veggie burgers, chicken breasts (without the skin), and fish.

Also, use cooking methods that do not add more calories to food such as broiling, steaming, and baking.

Eat grains like oatmeal, pasta, and rice. Practice how to balance days with high and low-calorie intakes with that of physical activity.

Remember, this phase only starts if the person is already equipped with the knowledge and strategies to live healthily. Also, this phase starts when the dieter is already capable of controlling portions and cravings, as well as capable of making the right food choices.

The main goal of Phase Two is to put strategies learned in Phase One into practice. Build eating habits that lead to a healthier life to achieve long-term, effective weight maintenance.

In Phase Two, the dieter has a choice in whether to continue the meal plan in Phase 1 or to continue the weight loss at his or her own pace. Support is still available. Weekly follow-up phone calls are made by the staff. These calls serve as coaching sessions with exercise physiologists and dietitians. They want to make sure that weight loss is sustained. It may be difficult to put the strategies into practice and these people are available to help out to make sure the dieter overcomes these difficulties and eventually succeeds. Also, these coaching sessions help to encourage accountability.

In-Clinic HMR

The HMR program is also available as an in-clinic option. It is an available option to over 200 hospitals in the US, along with private medical clinics and other similar facilities. For in-clinic, HMR combines structured diets with education on lifestyle and group support, along with HMR foods designed for weight loss. Depending on the need and the overall health condition, some HMR plans incorporate medical supervision.

Decision-Free Diet

Generally, if a person has to lose more than 40 pounds, rapid and most effective weight loss is achieved through a Decision-Free diet. Under this program, the calorie intake is very low. The dieter will only eat around 500 to 800 calories each day. This is a very low amount compared to the recommended 1,200 calories at least. Participants of this type of HMR program will only eat HMR products- no fruits or vegetables.

HMR Nutritional Information

A few other things to know about the HMR diet program include the following:

Conformity to the Dietary Guidelines

One of the main concerns in the HMR diet is the very low-calorie intake. Here's a breakdown of the nutrients that a participant gets during the program:

Fat – HMR meals are low in fat. Daily fat intake in HMR is well below the government recommendation of 20-35% of daily calories coming from fat. Typical daily fat intake under HMR is just 14%.

Protein – Protein intake in the diet is well within the recommended dietary guidelines. The recommendation is at 10 to 35% and the HMR typical meal provides 13%.

Carbohydrates – The recommended daily intake of carbohydrates is 45 to 66% of the daily calories. In HMR, carbohydrate intake is slightly higher. Typical meals in a day will provide about 67% of carbohydrates.

Salt – Most people consume too much salt. It comes from almost every food. The daily recommended maximum intake is only 2,300 milligrams and below. For those with high-risk profiles (e.g., hypertensive, African-American, with chronic kidney diseases, or diabetic), the daily maximum salt intake is limited to 1,500 mg. A typical HMR diet provides 1,967 mg of salt, falling well below the daily maximum for the average person. For more restrictive HMR diet types, the salt content of the meals becomes much higher.

The above nutrients are just some of the most common nutrient concerns when it comes to weight loss diets. Aside from these, HMR incorporates other key ingredients that help in improving weight loss and keep the body healthy, too. The following key nutrients are considered in the 2010 Dietary Guidelines as "nutrients of concern" because a lot of people do not get enough of these.

Fiber – The dietary daily recommended intake of fiber for adults is 22 to 34 grams- an amount that a lot of people rarely get enough of. Fiber helps to feel full and promotes a better digestive process. Major sources of dietary fiber are whole grains, vegetables, beans, and fruits. These are all encouraged in the HMR diet. A typical daily HMR menu would provide about 13 grams of fiber.

Potassium – According to the 2010 Dietary Guidelines, getting enough potassium in the daily diet can help counter the negative effects of sodium in the body such as raised blood pressure levels. Potassium also reduces the rate of bone loss and the risk of the development of kidney stones. The majority of the population consumes far too much sodium and far too little potassium.

The recommended daily intake is 4,700mg. Bananas are the most popular potassium source, but one needs to eat about 11 pieces a day just to supply the daily requirement. There are other food sources too such as apricots. In HMR, a typical daily meal consisting of HMR pre-packaged food can supply 1,920mg- a little short of the daily requirement. But, remember that fruits and vegetables are a must-add to HMR foods. Vegetables and fruits are naturally rich sources of potassium. With this, a dieter under the HMR program is very likely to reach the recommended daily intake of potassium.

Calcium – This mineral is not just for healthy bones. It is also important in a lot of vital functions such as good heart contraction, good function of the blood vessels, and better muscle action. The recommendation for daily calcium intake is 1,000 to 1,300 mg. A typical HMR daily menu provides an average of 1,515 mg- well above the recommended range.

Vitamin B12 – In a day, adults should take about 2.4 micrograms of vitamin B12. This vitamin is essential for cellular metabolism to proceed properly. Great sources are fish such as trout and salmon. Yogurt and eggs are excellent vitamin B12 sources, too. A typical HMR daily meal provides 6.3 micrograms.

Vitamin D – The daily recommendation for vitamin D intake in adults is 15 micrograms. It can be obtained through sunlight exposure but sadly, most people still don't get enough. A 3-ounce piece of sockeye salmon contains almost 20 micrograms- more than enough to supply the daily vitamin D requirement. A typical HMR diet provides, even more, about 126 micrograms.

How Much Does HMR Cost

HMR has several different options for you to choose from for both in-clinic and in-home. For some of the providers, in-home options may cost up to $199.95 for the first 3 weeks. The plan is inclusive of the following:

- 48 servings of HMR 120 Shake mix.
- 42 assorted HMR Entrees
- 1 packet of HMR 70 Plus Pudding or a mix to sample
- Support Guides and weekly group coaching by phone and many more.

After 3 weeks of the first shipment, you will likely get another shipment for $180. You will also be responsible for buying your fruits and vegetables.

Bars are also an additional cost and there are also very many additional meal replacements that you are going to incur a cost on.

Exercise

This is one of the necessities for those on the HMR. However, those who are starting on this don't have to start exercising. You are later supported to hit 2,000 calories every week. For this reason, just make sure you choose the best exercise for the whole process.

Start working towards this goal. After the first phase, you are supposed to burn at least 2000 calories a day through exercise.

End Results

If you choose the at-home solution, you can expect an average weight loss of 23 pounds during the first 12 weeks. You are likely to lose an additional 5 pounds if you are persistent and move to 26 weeks.

However, just note that results can vary. The above results are based on the average amount of weight that people who go for the home solution achieve within the weekly limit.

The results can be appealing if on an in-clinic. If this is your option, you are likely to achieve up to 47 pounds of weight loss within 12 weeks. However, this is one of the most effective and the most expensive options to go for.

A healthy life is a good thing that everyone should run for. Weight can impact the quality of life you live significantly and hence you should lead a healthy life by simply reducing weight. HMR is one of those best dietary plans that will help you reduce weight and avoid weight gain.

Is It Worth It?

Overall, the HMR program has a lot of benefits.

This is a diet plan that works perfectly for people who don't enjoy meal prepping and like the convenience of a pre-built program with support from mentors and coaches.

Prepped meals are convenient. You can just add it to your favorite product. It is also convenient for times when you are trying to pack lunch for a trip or work.

HMR saves you the hassle of planning every meal yourself and the exercises you need to do. As we all know, crafting the perfect diet plan can be a daunting task.

However, this leaves you with limited food choices. This might be a problem for some, but for those who want to lose weight fast, this can be overcome. Remember that just like in achieving any goal, discipline, and commitment are must-haves.

Another consideration is that this program does cost a nontrivial amount of initial investment, so for someone who is budget-conscious, this program might not be the best fit.

Another thing to consider is your lifestyle and habits. Because of the restrictive nature of the diet plan, people who have a very active social life may find this program very challenging.

Moreover, since this is a very low-calorie diet, this might be challenging for people with strenuous jobs. Naturally, we need calories to fuel our bodies. If your job requires you to move a lot, think carefully if you can commit to this diet.

Hopefully, by now, this beginner's overview has provided you with enough information to consider as you formulate your decision on whether to pursue this diet program or not.

Ultimately, it comes down to your goals. If weight loss is of great importance to you, and you have the funds set aside to invest in this program and the discipline to follow through, this program could be beneficial on your road to weight loss.

However, if you have certain lifestyle limitations as mentioned above, or you would still like to conduct more research on other plans available, then perhaps you can hold off on this program for a later time.

Correcting Misconceptions and Addressing FAQs

In the previous chapters, in-depth discussions on HMR—what it is, what to expect, how and why it works, how much it costs, and who it is for—were laid out. Practical tips were also given as to how you can go about the HMR diet.

Now, it is time to recap some important points by setting the records straight on misconceptions and frequently asked questions.

1. Is HMR effective?

As with any diet, the effect of HMR rests solely on your will to lose weight. Study the diet carefully; stick to the meal plan, and communicate with your diet coach. If you do, there will be a higher chances of you getting your desired weight.

The fact that you have decided to read this guide means you are dedicated to knowing more about it. You are one step closer to being able to maximize the potential of HMR!

2. Do I need to consult with a health professional before trying HMR?

It is entirely up to you. It is not a requirement since joining the HMR program includes having mentors like diet coaches to aid you in your weight loss journey. These coaches are knowledgeable about HMR, as well as health and nutrition. However, if you prefer checking with a dietitian or nutritionist from a hospital you are familiar with before committing to the program, that will be fine too.

3. Can I do the HMR program alone?

You definitely can, but there might be times when you will feel lonely eating a different meal than everyone else. To avoid this, it is recommended that people undergoing the HMR diet communicate with a support group. Aside from talking to a diet coach, you can be introduced to a community that, just like you, is doing the HMR diet. Knowing you are not alone, and having other people acting as your accountability partners in this endeavor makes a lot of difference.

4. I have medical conditions. Can I still push through with HMR?

Yes, you can, but be mindful of possible repercussions. An assessment will be given by a diet coach before moving forward with the program. It is best to be transparent about your medical history to make your weight loss journey safe, healthy, and smooth sailing.

5. What if I realize I cannot do it halfway?

The reason why a diet coach and a community are introduced to you is to ensure you would be able to address your concerns and have a support system. However, it is understandable that a certain diet is not fit for everyone. Should you meet difficulties and decide to quit halfway, talk to your diet coach right away.

6. Can I still be healthy given that I will be consuming meal replacement shakes?

Yes, you can and you will be. HMR is backed with medical studies so it is designed to make you healthily lose weight.

Keep in mind though that you will not be consuming meal replacement shakes all the time. Meal replacement shakes are there to control your calorie intake for important meals of the day. Fruits and vegetables are allowed. Over time, you will also be guided by your diet coach to transition to healthy meals so you can consume fewer meal-replacement shakes.

7. I am on the HMR diet. Do I still need to exercise?

Yes, you do. Diets are all about lifestyle changes. Physical activities are still needed to aid your weight loss and to strengthen your body.

8. I have a normal weight and body mass index, but I want to eat better. Is the HMR diet for me?

HMR is originally designed for those in need to lose a big amount of weight. If you are within the normal range of weight and body mass index, you should consult with a health professional first if HMR is for you.

Remember that everyone responds differently to each type of diet. Whether HMR is for you or not will depend on the state of your body and the assessment given by a diet coach.

9. I am on a budget. How do I do the HMR program?

The HMR program can be quite expensive for some at almost $200 for the first three weeks. Before coming up with the decision, though, try to compute your food expenses.

Consider how much you spend when you go for groceries, eat in restaurants, order food delivery, and purchase in coffee shops. If your expenses would tally to roughly $200 for three weeks, then diverting that amount to the HMR diet and shifting to a healthier lifestyle would not be so bad, right?

10. How long will it take me to get my desired weight?

There is no definite timeline when it comes to weight loss. The weight you shed can range from 23 to 47 pounds for the first twelve weeks. The length of the HMR program varies from person to person depending on the desired weight and progress. One thing is for sure: be mindful of your food intake and exercise, and you will be on the right track.

11. Is the HMR program sustainable in getting long-term results?

As with any diet, the result of the HMR program, whether short-term or long-term, is reliant on you. The idea for the HMR program is not just to lose weight through meal replacement shakes, but to help you become more aware of what you eat.

People often think that everything ends at phase one, which is when they lose the most weight. What they do not realize is that phase two, which is less structured, is more important.

Phase two transitions the usual food in your diet. It gives you an idea of how your daily food intake should be. By learning more about calorie intake and meal preparation in phase two, the HMR program becomes more sustainable for long-term weight loss or weight maintenance.

Conclusion

HMR is among the many diet options available nowadays. What sets it apart, however, is that it was originally designed by medical professionals to help obese people lose weight. Given this, it is important to look at it objectively while evaluating your lifestyle.

How much weight do you want and need to lose? What made you want to embark on a weight loss journey? What are you prepared to do to achieve your target weight? These are things that you should ask yourself before everything else. Your answers will keep you anchored as you go through your diet.

There is no single fail-proof way to lose weight. Each diet has its pros and cons. With HMR, the idea is to build momentum and inspiration from weight loss jump-start through this program to shift to a better lifestyle. This is why it was divided into phases that transition from a restrictive diet that is hinged on meal replacement into a more lenient one that incorporates mainstream food.

There are many disciplines needed to push through with a structured and seemingly rigid diet like HMR. It is convenient in terms of having minimal meal preparation. It is exciting in the sense that you will be able to meet new people who are on the same page as you are. As you move forward with the program, however, you will be given more freedom in terms of your diet. The challenge is this: will you be able to maintain it when you are no longer restricted to meal replacement shakes and nutrition bars?

At the end of the HMR program, the goal is not only to get your desired weight with the help of mentors like diet coaches, and the community that was built around it but to develop a healthy lifestyle that will help you sustain your progress.

References and Helpful Links

HMR program | U.S. News Best Diets - US News Health. (n.d.). Retrieved May 6, 2023, from https://health.usnews.com/best-diet/hmr-program.

HMR Weight Management | Trinity Health Michigan. (n.d.). Retrieved May 6, 2023, from https://www.trinityhealthmichigan.org/find-a-service-or-specialty/nutrition-weight-management-and-bariatrics/programs/hmr-weight-management/.

How much weight you can expect to lose in HMR if you stay "in the box": Scott D. Isaacs, MD: endocrinologist. (n.d.). Retrieved May 6, 2023, from https://www.atlantaendocrine.com/blog/how-much-weight-you-can-expect-to-lose-in-hmr-if-you-stay-in-the-box.

The HMR diet: Weight management plan reviews, cost, foods, and more. (2021, April 20). EverydayHealth.Com. https://www.everydayhealth.com/diet-nutrition/the-hmr-diet-weight-management-plan-reviews-cost-foods-and-more/.

Why you shouldn't try this fad diet for fast weight loss. (n.d.). LIVESTRONG.COM. Retrieved May 6, 2023, from https://www.livestrong.com/article/13723868-hmr-program/.

www.ingramcontent.com/pod-product-compliance
Lightning Source LLC
LaVergne TN
LVHW051925060526
838201LV00062B/4698